A little book of serpents

by Yvonne Aburrow

Birdberry Books
Oxford

Contents

Minoan Snake Goddess from the Palace at Knossos, Crete

Adder

Varieties

The *Viperidae* (Vipers) include the Common Viper (*Vipera berus*); the Asp Viper (*Vipera aspis*), a very venomous snake found in Europe; the Levantine Viper (*Vipera lebetina*); the Desert or Orsini's Viper (*Vipera ursinii*) and the Long-nosed or Sand Viper (*Vipera ammodytes*), both found in southern Europe; the Carpet or Saw-scaled Viper (*Echis carinatus*), found in desert regions of Africa and India; the deadly Daboia, Tic-Polonga, or Russell's Viper (*Vipera russelli*), found in India, Sri Lanka, Burma, and Thailand; the Gaboon Viper (*Bitis gabonica*), from the forests of equatorial Africa; and the Puff Adder (*Bitis arietans*), from the region south of the Sahara, whose bite can be fatal. The *Crotalinae* (Pit Vipers) include the Water Moccasin or Cottonmouth (*Agkistrodon piscivorus*) from the swamps of North America; the Copper-head Snake (*Agkistrodon contortrix*) from the forests of North America; the Siberian Moccasin (*Agkistrodon halys caraganus*) from the steppes of central Asia; the Fer-de-Lance (*Bothrops atrox*) from Central and South America; the Urutu (*Bothrops alternatus*), from the jungles of South America; and the Rattlesnakes, of which there are about fifteen species, found only on the American continent. They are called rattlesnakes because they have a loosely jointed section of dried skin at the end of their tails which they erect and shake when disturbed, making a rattling sound. The most common species are the Sidewinder or Horned Rattlesnake (*Crotalus cerastes*) and the Prairie Rattlesnake (*Crotalus viridis helleri*).

Folklore

In Christianity, the viper is one of the four aspects of the devil, according to St Augustine. The deaf adder depicts sinners who close their ears to Christian doctrine.

Mythology

The viper was one of the Eleven Mighty Helpers enlisted by Tiamat in her fight against Marduk.

In Scotland, various stones were reputed to have healing powers. Among them were adder stones (*a Chlach Nathrach*), also known as druidical beads, which are sometimes found in the heather. A man from the Isle of Lewis told F. Marian McNeill that the adders form themselves into a knot and move round and round on a stone until a hole is worn. They then writhe through the hole one after the other, and leave slime on it, which eventually becomes hard. It is this which gives the stone its healing virtues. Serpent stones were used to ease the pains of child-bed, as protection from enchantment, for general healing, and as weights for the distaff.

Asp

The asp is found in North Africa, Egypt, Arabia, and Southern Europe. The *Elapidae* have poison fangs in the front part of the upper jaw. They include the cobras, such as the Indian or Spectacled Cobra (*Naja naja*), the Monocled Cobra (*Naja naja kaouthia*), the smaller Asian Cobra (Naja naja oxiana) and the King Cobra (*Ophiophagus hannah*), all of which live in Asia. The Asp or Egyptian Cobra (*Naja haje*) lives in Africa. Another species of Elapid is the Banded Krait (*Bungarus fasciatus*), which lives in south-east Asia.

Symbolism

In Egypt, the asp was the symbol of the Sun, royalty, dominion, and power. The uraeus, which consisted of a solar disk supported by two asps, symbolised sovereignty, royalty, power, light, life and death, the power to rule, the destruction of enemies, and the eye of Ra, the Sun god. The so-called 'horned asp' may well have been the slug (q.v.).

In Greece, it embodied protective and benevolent power.

Chameleon

Varieties

Chameleons are arboreal climbing lizards. The Common Chameleon (*Chamaeleo chamaeleon*) is the only species of the *Chamaeleontidae* found in Europe, in the south of Spain and some of the Mediterranean islands. It is also found in North Africa, Arabia, Syria, and Asia Minor. Other species live in Africa, Madagascar, India, and Sri Lanka. The Common Chameleon lays eggs, but some of the other species give birth to live young.

Folklore

Some African peoples regard the chameleon as a magical animal and a rain-bringer. It can use its eyes independently of each other, so it is said to be able to see into the future and the past. Its spherical eyeballs are hidden behind fused eyelids with a small central opening.

Mythology

The chameleon was the sacred animal of the Dahomey mother goddess, Lissa, who was the mother of the Sun god Maou and the Moon god Gou.

The Bantu god Unkulunkulu sent a chameleon to tell humans they were immortal, but the chameleon lingered, so he sent a lizard to tell them they were mortal. The lizard arrived first, so humanity became mortal.

Symbolism

The chameleon represents the element of Air; it was believed to be nourished by the wind. It also symbolises the Four Elements. Its changing colour is a symbol of inconstancy and mobile fortunes.

In Christianity, the chameleon symbolises the devil taking diffrent disguises to deceive humanity.

Crocodile

Varieties

Crocodiles belong to the subclass Archosauria. The Nile Crocodile (*Crocodylus niloticus*) lives in the rivers of Northern and Central Africa and Madagascar. The Gharial (*Gavialis gangeticus*) lives in the Ganges, Indus, and Brahmaputra rivers in India, and was once regarded as sacred by the Hindus. The Broad-fronted Crocodile (*Osteolaemus tetraspis*) lives in equatorial West Africa; it does not attack humans. Related species are the Caiman, found in South America, and the American Alligator (*Alligator mississipiensis*), which lives in the Mississippi River in the south-eastern part of North America.

Folklore

In ancient times, the crocodile was thought to have no tongue, and was therefore used as a symbol of silence.

Travellers' tales related that crocodiles moan and sigh like a person in distress to lure humans to the river bank, then devour them. They are even reputed to shed tears over the prey whilst eating it, hence the expression "crocodile tears", a symbol of hypocrisy.

Mythology

In Egypt, the crocodile was sacred to a number of deities. It was an attribute of Set, depicting his brutality and evil. Sebek was crocodile-headed, and symbolised vicious passions, deceit, dissimulation, hypocrisy, and treachery. He was the god of the Fayoum, an ancient crocodile clan, and the son of the goddess Neith. He swallowed the Moon, then wept. Sebek was later identified with both Ra and Set, and was known to the Greeks as Souchos or Petesuchos, the Greek version of an Egyptian name meaning 'the one who belongs to Sebek'. Petesuchos was a sacred crocodile and the incarnation of Sebek. Sebek's most important shrines were at Crocodilopolis (called Arsinoe after the time of Ptolemy II). The sacred beast lived in a lake near the temple, and wore golden rings in his ears. Devotees riveted bracelets to his forelegs. Other sacred crocodiles were the family of Sebek. The crocodile was also sacred to Apep and Serapis, and was depicted at the feet of Ptah. Apep was the snake-god, lord of the powers of darkness, and a manifestation of Set. He was the serpent that threatened Osiris' Boat of Millions of Years as it sailed through the Underworld. Ptah was the creator, smith, and potter god who made the Cosmic Egg on his potter's wheel. The goddess Sekhmet was occasionally depicted as crocodile-headed. She represented the fierce and destructive aspect of the Sun. Taueret, the hippopotamus goddess, who presided over pregnancy and childbirth, and rebirth, had the tail of a crocodile.

In central Africa, there is a venerable crocodile called Lutembi, who comes to the shore of Lake Victoria-Nyanza, where the fishermen give him fish.

In Australian Aborigine mythology the Rainbow Snake Women are the offspring of the Rainbow Serpent and crocodiles. They entice men to their deaths with sweet songs and honeyed words. Protection from them may be obtained from red ochre from caves, which represents the Earth Mother's menstrual blood.

Symbolism

The crocodile symbolises the passage through the realms of death in order to be reborn. Being swallowed by a crocodile is likened to a descent into hell. With its mouth open, it represents going against the current, which portrays freedom from conformity. In some traditions, it is the guardian of the threshold. Like other amphibians, it represents spirit and matter, the dual nature of humanity. It also represents the fertility of the waters.

In psychoanalysis, the shadow is the first figure to emerge from the unconscious, and according to Jung, it often poses a *quaestio crocodilina*, because it is a guardian of the threshold. The story goes that a crocodile stole a child from its mother. The mother asked it to give the child back, but the crocodile replied that it would only do so if she could give a true answer to its question, "Shall I give the child back?" Whether she replies Yes or No, the answer is untrue, so in either case she doesn't get the child back.

Dinosaur

Varieties

There were many varieties of dinosaur, some of which have evolved into modern reptiles and birds. Some of the most famous are the brontosaurus (thunder lizard), the triceratops, the plesiosaur, the pterodactyl, the tyrannosaurus rex, and the ichthyosaur. The fossilised remains of an ichthyosaur were discovered by Mary Bush at Lyme Regis in the nineteenth century, as a result of which she became a famous fossil collector.

Folklore

It was once thought that the remains of dinosaurs which were occasionally uncovered were the bones of dragons.

Mythology

The Loch Ness Monster is believed to be a surviving dinosaur. If it exists, however, there would have to be more than one, in order for it to be able to breed.

Symbolism

The dinosaur symbolises anything that has been out-evolved by something else, also large and unwieldy organisations, technology, or ideas.

Lizard

Order	Squamata (Scaly Reptiles)
Sub-order	Lacertilia (Lizards)

Varieties

Lizards and snakes belong to the subclass of reptiles called the Lepidosauria, of which all except one species belong to the order Squamata. The *Lacertidae* (True Lizards) include the Sand Lizard (*Lacerta agilis*), which is the most common lizard of central Europe; the Wall Lizard (*Lacerta muralis*), mostly found in the Mediterranean region, but also in western and central Europe; the Green Lizard (*Lacerta viridis*), found in southern and central Europe; and the Common or Viviparous Lizard (*Lacerta vivipara*), whose young hatch in the female's body in northern and central Europe, but from eggs in the Pyrenees. The Common lizard is sometimes found as far north as the Arctic Circle. The *Scincidae* (Skinks) include the Snake-eyed Skink (*Ablepharus kitaibelii*), found mostly in south-eastern Europe. There are about three hundred species of Geckos (*Gekkonidae*), which are small climbing lizards. The Agamidae family includes the Indian Bloodsucker (*Calotes versicolor*), so called because the throat of the male swells and reddens when it fights another male during the mating season; the Spiny-tailed Lizard (*Uromastix acanthinurus*), which lives in the Middle East; and the Agama (*Agama sanguinolenta*), which lives on the steppes of Central Asia. The Iguanidae include the Green Iguana (*Iguana iguana*), which lives in the tropical regions of America; the Chuckwalla (*Sauromalus obesus*) from the deserts of Arizona and the south-west; and the American Basilisk (*Basiliscus americanus*). The *Cordylidae* (Girdle-tailed Lizards) include the Armadillo Lizard (*Cordylus cataphractus*) of Central and South Africa. The *Anguidae* (Slow-worms) have no limbs and are often mistaken for Snakes. The Slow-worm (*Anguis fragilis*) is said to live to over fifty years old. Another member of this family is the Glass-snake or Scheltopusik (*Ophisaurus apodus*), which lives in southern Europe and central Asia. It was formerly believed that all lizards were poisonous, but this is only true of the *Helodermatidae*, which live in the deserts of Mexico and the southern states. These include the Gila Monster (*Heloderma suspectum*). The *Varanidae* (Monitors) are carnivorous lizards found in India, central Asia, North Africa, Arabia, Iran, and western India. The chameleon (q.v.) is also a species of lizard.

Folklore

The lizard was believed to have no tongue and to feed only on dew. Because of this, it was a symbol of silence. The Romans believed that the lizard slept through the winter, so to them it symbolised death and resurrection. In Roman art, the lizard was often depicted with sleeping cupids.

In a Santal folktale, a man was lying asleep when his soul became very thirsty and left his body in the form of a lizard. It got into a pitcher of water, but someone put the lid back on before it could return to his body. Just as his friends were preparing to cremate him, someone lifted the lid off the pitcher, and the lizard-soul was able to return. When the man asked his friends why they were weeping, they told him that they had thought him dead. He explained that he had gone down a well to get water but had been unable to get out.

Mythology

The Araucanian people of Chile have a god of winds called Meuler who is depicted as a lizard.

The Bantu god Unkulunkulu sent a chameleon to tell humans they were immortal, but the chameleon lingered, so he sent a lizard to tell them they were mortal. The lizard arrived first, so humanity became mortal. In some parts of Africa the lizard was believed to be able to transform itself into a leopard, a lion or a hyena. It can be a totem animal, but may also have a sinister aspect.

In Australian mythology, the lizard Tarrotarro is a culture hero. He divided humanity into two genders and taught the people the arts. In Polynesian mythology, Moko, the King of the Lizards, protects fishing. In Maori mythology, the lizard pulled the first human from the waters of creation. In Hawaii, there are lizard gods who are both animal ancestor figures and tutelary spirits. There was a stone temple in Tahiti dedicated to a lizard god. The lizard was regarded as the guardian of the soul in the body.

To the people of the Amazon River, the lizard is a manifestation of the Lord of Animals and Fish. It is also the messenger of the god who told men they were mortal.

In Central America, the desert peoples believe the lizard to be a form of the Great Spirit.

In Europe, the lizard is generally regarded as a sinister creature, because it was thought to be venomous. Shakespeare used this idea in both Macbeth, where a lizard's leg was an ingredient of the witches' cauldron, and *Henry VI Part II*, Act III, Scene II).

Symbolism

In ancient Egypt and Greece, the lizard symbolised divine wisdom and good fortune; it also averted evil. It appears with other creatures on the votive Hand of Sabazios. It was also sacred to Hermes and Serapis.

In both Zoroastrianism and christianity, the lizard symbolises evil. In Zoroastrianism, it represents Ahriman; in christianity, it represents the devil.

Poetry

"I am the Lizard King
I can do anything..."

Jim Morrison

Python

Varieties

The Pythons lay eggs. The Indian Python (*Python molurus*) lives in India, Sri Lanka, Malaya, and Indonesia.

Mythology

The python is an attribute of Apollo. Pytho was the name of the huge serpent which hatched from the mud of the deluge, which was slain by Apollo at Delphi. Hence Apollo with a python symbolises the Sun overcoming darkness. Apollo frees the sun from the powers of darkness and liberates the soul to find inspiration and knowledge. The python also represents the serpent of wisdom. The name python can also refer to Apollo, his priestess, or a frenzied person. In the Trojan wars, the death of Laocoön and his sons, who were killed by Apollo's python, made possible the entry of the wooden horse into Troy. Every four years, the Greeks held the Pythian Games near Delphi.

In West Africa, Zombie was the python god. His worship was taken to the Caribbean by the slaves, and he is still worshipped in some Voodoo ceremonies in Haiti and the Southern USA. The word zombie also means an undead person.

Symbolism

The python represents the powers of darkness and the feminine earth principle.

Snake

Rune	Ior
Sub-order	*Ophidia*
Constellations	Draco, Hydra

Varieties

There are many varieties of snake, some of which are poisonous, and some which are not. The main varieties in Britain are the Adder or Viper (*Vipera berus*) and the Grass Snake (*Natrix natrix*). The slow-worm is not a snake, but a form of lizard. In central Europe are found the Colubridae, which are non-poisonous snakes. These include the Grass Snake, the European Smooth Snake (*Coronella austriaca*), found inmost of temperate Europe and Asia, and the Tessellated Snake (*Natrix tessellata*), found in central and south-east Europe. Another member of the Colubridae family is the Dice Snake (*Natrix piscator*), found in south-east Asia. The European Whip Snake (*Coluber gemonensis*) lives in southern Europe and western Asia. The Oriental Rat Snake (*Ptyas mucosus*) lives in central and southern Asia. In North America, there are the Shovel-nose Snake (*Chionactis occipitalis annulata*), which lives in the Californian desert; the Mountain King Snake (*Lampropeltis zonata*), which lives in the western states; the Eastern Hog-nose Snake (*Heterodon platyrhinos*), in Florida and Texas. In India, the Long-nose Tree Snake (*Ahaetulla nasuta*) is a member of the Opistoglyph group of the *Colubridae*, which have poison fangs in the rear of the upper jaw which they only use to bite prey after they have seized it. Another member of this group is the Vine Snake (*Oxybelis acuminatus*), found in tropical regions of America.

The Boa Constrictor (*Constrictor constrictor*) is found in Brazil, Venezuela, and north-east Peru. There are various other members of the Boa family: the Emerald Tree Boa (*Coallus caninus*) is found in tropical South America; the Rainbow Boa (*Epicrates cenchria*) found in Central and South America; the Indian Sand Boa (*Eryx johnii*); and the largest true Boa, the Anaconda (*Eunectes murinus*) which can grow up to 20 feet long, and lives in the forests and swamps of northern Latin America. Boas give birth to live young. The Pythons, on the other hand, lay eggs. The Indian Python (*Python molurus*) lives in India, Sri Lanka, Malaya, and Indonesia.

The *Elapidae* have poison fangs in the front part of the upper jaw. They include the cobras, such as the Indian or Spectacled Cobra (*Naja naja*), the Monocled Cobra (*Naja naja kaouthia*), the smaller Asian Cobra (*Naja naja oxiana)* and the King Cobra (*Ophiophagus hannah*), all of which live in Asia. The Asp or Egyptian Cobra (*Naja haje*) lives in Africa. Another species of Elapid is the Banded Krait (*Bungarus fasciatus*), which lives in south-east Asia.

The *Viperidae* (Vipers) include the Common Viper (*Vipera berus*); the Asp Viper (*Vipera aspis*), a very venomous snake found in Europe; the Levantine Viper (*Vipera lebetina*); the Desert or Orsini's Viper (*Vipera ursinii*) and the Long-nosed or Sand Viper (*Vipera ammodytes*), both found in southern Europe; the Carpet or Saw-scaled Viper (*Echis carinatus*), found in desert regions of Africa and India; the deadly Daboia, Tic-Polonga, or Russell's Viper (*Vipera russelli*), found in India, Sri Lanka, Burma, and Thailand; the Gaboon Viper (*Bitis gabonica*), from the forests of equatorial Africa; and the Puff Adder (*Bitis arietans*), from the region south of the Sahara, whose bite can be fatal. The *Crotalinae* (Pit Vipers) include the Water Moccasin or Cottonmouth (*Agkistrodon piscivorus*) from the swamps of North America; the Copper-head Snake (*Agkistrodon contortrix*) from the forests of North America; the Siberian Moccasin (*Agkistrodon halys caraganus*) from the steppes of central Asia; the Fer-de-Lance (*Bothrops atrox*) from Central and South America; the Urutu (*Bothrops alternatus*), from the jungles of South America; and the Rattlesnakes, of which there are about fifteen species, found only on the American continent. They are called rattlesnakes because they have a loosely jointed section of dried skin at the end of their tails which they erect and shake when disturbed, making a rattling sound. The most common species are the Sidewinder or Horned Rattlesnake (*Crotalus cerastes*) and the Prairie Rattlesnake (*Crotalus viridis helleri*).

Folklore

It was once believed that if snakes were attacked they would swallow their young and not let them go until they reached a safe place. It was also believed that snakes could restore life to the dead or incarnate the soul of an ancestor. People kept snakes as pets in Greece, Rome and Crete as guardians and bringers of fertility and healing. It was also believed in ancient Greece that if a serpent licked your ears you would obtain the gift of prophecy. Cassandra and Helenus were said to be so gifted, because serpents licked their ears whilst asleep in the temple of Apollo. Snakes were also believed to be androgynous, and so represent self-creating deities and the generative power of the earth. It lives in holes in the ground and disappears into cracks in the ground, and hence are associated with the underworld. Being reptiles, they seem sinuous and mysterious, and as cold-blooded animals, they seem remote from human emotion. Snakes were associated with fertility, and it was anciently believed that snakes could have intercourse with women and make them pregnant. In some places it was believed that a snake's bite caused girls' first menstruation, and that women were more likely to have intercourse with serpents when menstruating. For thi reason women were not allowed to go to springs or into the bush during menstruation in case they became pregnant by the snake. (In other places the same legend is associated with fish.) If a spring is inhabited by a sacred snake, women may go there on purpose to become pregnant.

In the Punjab, the Mirasan people carried a snake made of dough from house to house at the end of August, and people made offerings of corn or dough to it. When all the houses had been visited, the dough snake was buried, and a small grave was erected over it. During the nine-day festival in September, the women would go to the grave to worship and make offerings of curds to the snake. What ws left over would be taken home and given to their children. In areas where there were a lot of real snakes, the curds would be carried into the forest and left there for the snakes. A member of the Mirasan tribe would not kill a snake, and its bite could not hurt them. If they found a dead snake, they would dress it and give it a full funeral.

The snake is associated with the Moon because of its ability to change or renew its skin, which is similar to the Moon's waxing and waning. Both the Moon and the snake are associated with immortality, and the legendary soma drink (which bestows immortality) is brewed from the Moon tree. The knowledge of it is given by the serpent which lives in the tree.

In a Chinese folktale, White Snake (*bai she*) turns herself into a beautiful young woman, falls in love with a young man, and makes him rich. A Buddhist monk persuades him that she is evil, and despite the fact that she is now carrying his child, they confine her to a pagoda. Eventually the son grows up to be a celebrated scholar, and returns to visit and honour his snake-mother.

In an old folk remedy, it was customary to wrap a snakeskin around the head as a cure for a headache. Folklore also held that the snake had a jewel in its head.

Mythology

According to Greek myth, Hermes made the caduceus by using his staff to separate two serpents that were fighting, so it symbolises peace. The two serpents also represent healing and poison, health and illness, binding and loosing, good and evil, fire and water, ascent and descent. Together, they represent equilibrium, wisdom, and fertility. In Alchemy, they are the masculine sulphur and the feminine quicksilver. They represent the powers of transformation, sleeping and waking, the dissolution and coagulation processes within the Great Work, the synthesis of opposites, and mediation between the upper and lower realms.

The caduceus also corresponds to the Kabbalistic Tree of Life (Ets Chaim), since the winged sun at the top can represent the Ain Soph, the left-hand snake is the Pillar of Severity, the staff is the Pillar of Clemency, and the right-hand snake is the Pillar of Mercy. Each of their coils about the staff delineates one of the Four Worlds (Aziluth, the World of Emanation; Beriah, the World of Creation; Yezirah, the World of Formation; and Asiyyah, the World of Action).

In Alchemy, the serpent was regarded as the embodiment of Fire:

> "The body of the Serpent tells you it is a fierie substance, for a Serpent is full of heat and fire, which made the Egyptians esteem him divine: this appears by his quick motion without feet or finns, much like that of the Pulse, for his impetuous hot spirit shoots him on like a Squid. There is also another Analogie, for the Serpent receives his youth, so strong is his natural heat, and casts off his old skin. Truly the matter is a very Serpent, for she renews herself in a thousand ways."
>
> (from "*Magia Adamica*" by Thomas Vaughan)

The serpent on a staff is the fixation of quicksilver, the sublimation of the vital force. A serpent passing through a circle is the alchemical fusion.

The Greeks and Romans regarded the serpent as a guardian spirit, and it was often depicted as such on their altars. At Athens, in the temple of Athena, they kept a serpent believed to be the reincarnation of Erichthonius in a cage, and it was called the guardian spirit of the temple. According to legend, Alexander the Great was fathered upon Olympia by Jupiter Ammon in the form of a snake. Snakes were also sacred to Demeter, with corn and poppies, because they were associated with initiation, and probably appeared in the Eleusinian Mysteries, possibly as part of a ritual of mystical union. The temple at Eleusis had a snake called Kychreus. They were also associated with saviour deities in the mystery religions (such as Orpheus). Demeter placed snakes at the river Styx after Poseidon had tricked her into mating with him in the form of a horse (she was a mare at the time); this may be symbolic of a distinction between fresh water and the salt sea, sacred to Poseidon. The snake was sacred to Zeus Cthonios. The python at Delphi was sacred to Apollo after he slew it; it was originally the attribute of the Earth Goddess. The shrine of Apollo at Spireus had a sacred snake which was tended by a naked virgin. The Pelasgians said that they were descended from the cosmic serpent Ophion and the goddess Eurynome (one of the Oceanids). The chimaera (see mythical animals) had a serpent's tail. Its mother was Echidne, a winter snake-goddess, and its father was Typhon, the storm-god. Typhon himself was a snake-headed giant. He was the god of storms, created by Hera in her rage at Athene being born from Zeus' forehead. He lived in a cave on Mount Parnassus. He was identified with Set when the Hyksos invaders colonised Egypt around 1320-1200 bce. He is sometimes confused with Typhœus, the son of Gaea and Uranus, whose lower body consisted of coiled serpents. Snakes were often the personification of river deities, such as the River Acheloüs, which was a bull-headed snake, or capable of changing shape, first into a bull and then into a snake. Heracles wrestled with the snake, then it transformed itself into a bull, and he tore off one of its horns, which the nymphs threw into the river, where it became the Cornucopia (horn of plenty). Acheloüs was the son of Oceanus and Thetis and the brother of Nilus, according to Hesiod's Theogony. The Gorgons were the three daughters of Phorcys and his sister Ceto; they were winged monsters with serpents for hair. Euryale and Stheno were immortal, but Medusa was mortal, and was killed by Perseus. The winged horse, Pegasus, was born from her death-throes, though in some legends he was the result of her union with Poseidon. Medusa's head was then fixed to Athena's shield (which she had lent to Perseus), and he went on to kill the sea-serpent to which Andromeda was to be sacrificed. (The story is depicted in Edward Burne-Jones' Perseus Series, of which there are two versions, one in Southampton and one in Stuttgart.) According to one story, Medusa's hair was turned to serpents by Athene because she dared to claim equal beauty with her. Another Greek legend is that of Cadmus and Harmonia. Cadmus was sent by his father to look for his sister, who had been abducted by Zeus. On his journey, Cadmus stopped to make a libation to Zeus, and sent his companions in search of fresh water. Whilst drawing water from a spring in "an ancient forest which no axe had ever touched, and in the heart of it a cave, overgrown with branches and osiers", they disturbed the serpent of Mars, "a creature with a wonderful golden crest" whose eyes flashed with fire and whose body was full of poison, and it slew them all. When Cadmus went in search of them, he encountered the snake and slew it too. Then Pallas appeared to him and told him to sow its teeth in the earth. He did so, and warriors came fully formed from the earth. Many of them slew each other, but Pallas prevailed upon the last five to stop, and with these, Cadmus founded the city of Thebes, where he was married to Harmonia, the daughter of Mars and Venus. After a while they left Thebes and went to Illyria, where they became King and Queen, and were eventually turned into great serpents. The probable meaning of this is that they became identified with Illyrian snake deities. In Libya, they honoured the goddess Lamia, and she had a cult with orgiastic priestesses. In later Greek legend, she became a queen of Libya who was loved by Zeus and had her offspring taken away by Hera, who was jealous. In medieval legend, she became the Lamiae, beautiful demonesses who seduced and vampirised travellers and devoured children. Women with serpent hair (the Gorgons and the Erinnyes) represent powers of magic and sorcery. The underworld goddess Hecate was sometimes depicted with the the head of a snake or with snakes in her hair. In the legend of Jason, the people of Colchis gave him serpents' teeth to sow in the earth, which sprang up and grew into fierce warriors, but Jason threw a stone amongst them, whereupon they all turned on each other and killed one another. The snake was also a phallic symbol, and was therefore associated with ithyphallic deities such as Priapus, Pan and Pallas in the temples of lunar goddesses. Pan was worshipped in the temples of Selene, and Pallas and Priapus were worshipped in the temple of Vesta, the Roman hearth goddess. The priestesses of the Moon goddess were sometimes virgins, and sometimes offered their sexuality to the goddess in the Sacred Marriage (hieros gamos). Snakes were also kept in the temple of the Moon goddess.

For the Romans, snakes were associated with saviour divinities and deities of fertility and healing. They are also an attribute of Minerva as goddess of wisdom. The serpent was an attribute of Hercules, so the Romans identified him with a number of Celtic deities whose attributes were also serpents.

In Scandinavian mythology, the World Serpent, Jörmungand, coils about the rim of Midgard, containing the ocean. The god Loki was the father of the Midgard Serpent, the Fenris Wolf, and the goddess Hel. For causing Balder's death, Loki was bound to a rock with a snake dripping venom above him, but his wife Sigyn sits beside him catching the drips in a bowl. The Dread Biter, Niðhögg, lives at the foot of the World Tree, gnawing at its root.

The Celts connected the serpent with the healing waters and the Goddess Brighid. The horned or ram-headed serpent is connected with the Horned God, and he is depicted holding a ram-headed serpent on the Gundestrup cauldron. A relief from Meigle in Perthshire, Scotland, shows a bull-horned god with serpentine legs, who is accompanied by a bear and either a wolf or an otter. A relief found at Cirencester also depicts an antlered god with his legs as serpents which rear up beside him and end in a ram's head either side of his face. This may be a Roman or Belgic import, but could equally well have orginated with the Dobunni (the full Roman name of Cirencester was Corinium Dobunnorum). There are several altars with boars and serpents carved on them dedicated to Vitiris, a northern Celtic deity, whose name may mean 'the Mighty One'. It is possible that the warrior god and the horned god were conceived of as two separate beings, but they are both associated with serpents. The goddess of the River

Wharfe, Verbeia, may have been associated with snakes, as there is a relief of a goddess holding two snakes which has been identified with her. In any case, many aquatic cults incorporated the veneration of serpents. Borvo, the god of healing springs, is shown with a horned serpent rearing up at him. In the Mabinogion, in the story of the Lady of the Fountain, Owein witnesses a battle between a snake and a white lion. He kills the snake but takes the lion with him as a hunting companion. The Gaulish goddess Rosmerta was sometimes depicted with a caduceus, as she was the consort of Mercury in the synthesis of Roman and Celtic pantheons, especially in eastern Gaul. Epona was sometimes depicted with what appears to be a snake. A relief from Mavilly in France shows a snake coiling round an altar; on the other side is a goddess with two snakes in her left hand. Similarly, an altar found at Lypiatt Park in Gloucestershire has a snake carved in relief twining around it. A head wreathed in serpents represents fertility and protection. Snakes may also be malevolent in Celtic legend. In the epic of the Dindshenchas, there is a mighty snake which 'would have wasted all the cattle of the indolent hosts of Ireland by its doings', but that it was slain by the god Diancecht (the god of healing). It made three turns and sought to consume Diancecht, but he slew it. In the prose Dindshenchas, the warrior MacCecht slays Mechi, the son of the Morrigan (the raven and battle goddess). Mechi had three hearts with a serpent in each, which MacCecht burnt, scattering the ashes on the River Berba (now the River Barrow). Conall Cernach is regarded as the ancestor of the royal house of Dàl nAraide. He was a wandering champion, a warrior, headhunter, and guardian of boundaries. In the *Táin Bó Fraich* (Cattle Raid of Fraich) Conall Cernach, the hero of Ulster, attacked a castle guarded by a fearsome serpent, which submitted to him and slithered into his girdle. It was foretold that Conall Cernach would be able to destroy the fortress, which he does because his friend Fraech's wife and children are imprisoned within it. The acquiescence of the guardian serpent suggests that he may have been a deity similar to Cernunnos; the name is certainly similar.

In Slavonic mythology, the Syen are guardian spirits of the home who can enter the bodies of snakes, dogs, humans, and hens.

In France, the legendary lady Melusine had the form of a woman with two serpent tails. She appears in Irish, Scottish and French myth. In Poitou folklore, she was the wife of Raymond de Lusignan, whom she married on the condition that he never asked where she was on a Saturday, which was the day that she was transformed into a serpent. He eventually broke this condition, whereupon she grew wings and flew away weeping. This is a common theme in folklore, where the bride (or in some tales the groom) must retain an element of mystery for the marriage to be successful. In Basque legend, the husband of the goddess Mari is Sugaar, the serpent.

In Hinduism, essential spiritual energy is represented as the Kundalini, a white serpent lying coiled at the base of the spine in the muladhara-chakra. The adjective kundalin means circular, annulate, or coiled; kundalini is a feminine noun meaning serpent. The Kundalini lies dormant until it is awakened by yogic and/or spiritual practices. It then begins to ascend through the chakras, integrating the powers associated with each, until it reaches the highest point of awareness. The Kundalini is the primordial shakti, the sleeping serpent power of the psyche. Uncoiling the Kundalini serpent is to ascend to a mythical level of awareness, where enlightenment may be achieved. This process is analogous to the serpent shedding its skin, just as the Moon sheds her shadow. The Moon represents the light of immortal consciousness manifesting in the realm of space and time, and the kundalini reaching the sahasrara-padma (the crown chakra) is like the Full Moon, when its light is almost as powerful as the Sun's. The flickering tongue of the serpent shows the light within. The Kundalini is generally regarded as feminine, and a manifestation of the universal life force.

"The goddess is more subtle than the fibre of the lotus... She uncoils herself and raises Her head, and enters the royal road of the spine, piercing the mystic centres, until She reaches the brain. These things are not to be understood in a day... you taste Her nectar, and know that She is Life."

(a Tantric Yogini, quoted by Yeats-Brown in *Bengal Lancer*)

The serpent is also a manifestation of the fire god Agni, who is the fierce serpent; the dark serpent is the potentiality of fire. Vishnu rides on a cobra as the cosmic ocean, and sleeps on the coiled serpent of the waters. He is also accompanied by two nagas, with intertwined bodies, which represent the fertilised waters from which the Earth Goddess arises. Between incarnations he is cradled by the serpent Shesha, a thousand-headed serpent born from his mouth in his incarnation as Balarama, as he lay dying. The serpent also has a malefic aspect as Kaliya, which was vanquished by Krishna. He is often depicted dancing on the head of Kaliya. Another malefic serpent was Ahi, the throttler, a three-headed snake which was killed by Indra. Vritra, also slain by Indra, was another three-headed snake who imprisons the waters, causing drought, but may release them with his thunderbolt. The ruler of all snakes is the thousand-headed serpent Ananta, who represents infinity (his name means 'endless') and is coiled about the axis of the world, or floats on the Ocean of Milk, the mother of all life. Vishnu is sometimes depicted couched upon Ananta, and the serpent's energy gives him the impulse to dream the world into being. The sleep of Brahma is symbolised by two snakes, one with downward movement which represents the Divine Sleep, and one moving upward which represents the Divine Awakening. The lingam of Shiva is sometimes carved with a snake twining around it. The snake is one of the animals that supports the world in Hindu cosmology, along with the elephant, the tortoise, the bull, and the crocodile.

In Buddhism, the serpent is sometimes associated with the Buddha because he changed into a naga to heal the people. It is also one of the animals at the centre of the Round of Existence, where it represents anger.

In China, the serpent is a rain-bringer and a creator, and represents the fertilising power of the waters. It can also symbolise deceit, cunning, and sycophancy. It is the sixth animal of the Twelve Terrestrial Branches (the Chinese Zodiac). The brother and sister Fo-hi and Niu-kua are sometimes depicted as snakes with human heads, representing yin and yang. Hsuan-T'ien Shang-Ti (Supreme Lord of the Dark Heaven) is the enemy of evil spirits and demons, and the ruler of Water. He is depicted as a tall barefooted man with loose hair, standing on a turtle surrounded by a snake. From the period of the Warring States (500-250 bce) under the Chou Dynasty (1027-256 bce) comes a coiled bronze snake of 3½ turns, which closely resembles the sleeping kundalini serpent, which is also depicted as having 3½ turns. In the province of Guang-xi, there were believed to be snake deomns with human heads. If one of these called to you, it was best not to answer.

In Japan, the snake is the personification of Susanoo, the god of thunder and storms.

The rainbow is associated with the serpent in many cultures. In French, African, Indian, and indigenous American legends, the rainbow is a serpent which quenches its thirst in the sea. The African rainbow serpent encircles the Earth, and is a guardian of treasures. In Australia, the Rainbow Serpent can be male or female, and represents rain, water, and rivers, without which life could not be. Some areas regard the Rainbow Serpent as male, others as female. It causes rivers to flow to the sea, and is very important in the training of magicians. In Arnhem Land, the Rainbow Serpent is said to send a flood to destroy those who offend against the sacred lore. It is also associated with lightning. In the rites of the Fertility Mother in Arnhem Land, which take place just before the rainy season, you can hear the sound of the storm blowing through the Rainbow Serpent's horns. As the dancing and singing begins, it arches up into the sky. In the Kimberleys, it is associated with childbirth and the birth of spirit children. It is frequently depicted in Aborigine art. Some of their names for it are

Julunggui, Yurlunggui, or Wonambi. There are also Rainbow Snake Women, the offspring of the Rainbow Serpent and crocodiles, who entice men to their deaths with sweet songs and honeyed words. Protection from them may be obtained from red ochre from caves, which represents the Earth Mother's menstrual blood. In Victoria, there is a goddess called Karakarook, who descended to earth to defend women who were attacked by snakes when they were out digging for yams. She killed the snakes with a huge stick till it broke, then gave the pieces to the women.

In Maori mythology, the snake represents earthly wisdom, a worker in the swamp. In Oceanic mythology, the snake was a creator of the world, and is also associated with pregnancy. One some islands it is believed that the Cosmic Serpent lives underground and will eventually destroy the world. In Melanesian myth, the goddess Walutahanga (Eight Fathoms) is a huge guardian serpent, the provider of edible plants. In Fiji, Ngendei or Ngendel is the supreme god, who holds up the earth, causes earthquakes, and is lord of the dead and the father of comets. He is portrayed as half-man, half-snake.

In Algonquin and other forest peoples' mythology, snakes and aquatic creatures are believed to communicate with the powers of the underworld. In Iroquois and Huron myth, the Big Water Snake devours humanity, but is slain by Hino the Thunder Spirit and his warriors. The Great Manitou takes the form a serpent with horns when transfixing the Dark Manitou in the form of a toad. Onnioni is a horned snake god of Huron mythology whose horn could pierce mountains and rocks. Warriors carried pieces of his horn into battle to give them courage.

Jeff King was a medicine man of the Navaho (Dineh) people, who died aged about 110 in 1964. He produced pollen paintings, which he said were derived from a stone carving outside a cave 'on the east slope of a certain mountain'. The carving (and the paintings) portrayed two intertwined snakes with the heads facing east and west (similar to the Inca carving described below). The carving was unfortunately destroyed by water.

Among the Hopi, snakes are regarded as vital messengers. In the snake dance, they carry prayers. Before the ceremony, snakes are gathered (regardless of whether they are venomous or not). They are ceremonially purified with water and smoke (smudging), given cornmeal, and then released below the mesa to carry the people's prayers. There is no snake katsina (spirit) but there is a snake yom (clan). It is absolutely forbidden to eat snakes among the Hopi.

In Aztec mythology, Quetzalcoatl, the Feathered Serpent, is a god of the air and the Sun. He was the founder of agriculture, metallurgy, and other arts, associated with the east, fertility, life, the sun, wind, water, rain, thunder and lightning. He was said to have invented the calendar. He was particularly associated with the maize plant, which is interesting in that the Navaho (Dineh) sand painting of the ascent of the spirit depicts a pollen path climbing a maize stalk, which is analogous to the ascent of the kundalini up the sushumna. It is possible that his association with the serpent had a similar significance. He was driven out of Mexico by a superior deity (who apparently vanquished him by means of alcohol), and set sail in his magic boat for the land of Tlapallan. He was said to have been tall, pale-skinned, with long flowing hair and a beard. Hence the arrival of the Spaniards was initially greeted with enthusiasm by the indigenous peoples of Mexico. Another snake deity was Coatlicue, a woman with a skirt of snakes, who is also an Earth Mother and a lunar goddess. The snake was also the White God whose black bowels are the clouds from which the rain falls. A bird of prey dismembering a snake represents the birth of humanity, which was born from the blood of the snake. In this myth the snake represents the original uniformity of matter, which is differentiated by the coming of light in the form of the solar bird of prey. An Aztec codex written in the year 15 ce depicts an altar with two intertwined snakes facing in opposite directions. In Mayan mythology, Ixchel was the lunar goddess of disastrous floods, portrayed with a snake on her head, and Kukulcan (the feathered snake whose path is the waters) gave the calendar to humanity and was the patron of craftsmen; he was later merged with Quetzalcoatl. In Toltec mythology, the sky is symbolised by the sun god looking out of the jaws of a snake. The Incas had a deity called Urcaguay, the guardian of underground treasures, who was portrayed as a big snake with a deer's head, with his tail decorated with little gold chains.

The Araucanian Indians of Chile have a legend that if you sleep in the forest overnight, Pihuechenyi the winged snake will suck your blood.

In Egyptian mythology, Apep was the snake god, the lord of the powers of darkness. Every night Apep menaced the boat of the sun god, called the Boat of a Million Years. The boat was defended by the good serpent Mehen, which lived in the bows of the boat. The sun can only rise in the morning thanks to powerful spells of Tehuti. Apep is a manifestation of Set, and hence the enemy of the sun god and of the dead, who cannot return to life unless he is defeated. He was portrayed as a huge serpent called the Roarer. He was said to have been slain by Ra at the foot of Nut's sacred sycamore at Heliopolis. He sometimes attacks the sun god during the day, causing eclipses. In another myth Apep is defeated and bound by Selkhet, the scorpion goddess, whose husband was Nekhebkau, an underworld snake god with the limbs of a man. Another underworld dweller was the snake goddess Sati, who preyed on the dead (not to be confused with Satet). The two serpents either side of the solar disk (as seen in the crown of Horus) represent the two serpent goddesses who banished the enemies of Ra. Another ally of the sun god was Uraeus, a flame-breathing asp who destroyed Ra's enemies. Heh, the revealer of wisdom, was a serpent goddess. The snake goddess Buto manifested as a cobra. She may be the same as the serpent goddess Uto, who was called 'great in magic'. Rennutet was the snake goddess of the harvest and the ruler of the month of Pharmuthi. Mafdet, the lynx goddess, was famed as a killer of serpents, the lynx being a solar creature and the snake watery or cthonic. In the western desert, the snake god Ash was honoured; he was sometimes depicted with three heads, of a lion, a snake, and a vulture. The Ogdoad of Hermopolis were the first eight living beings created by Thoth (Tehuti). The males were frogs and the females were serpents, brought into being by the sound of Tehuti's voice. In the Graeco-Roman period of Alexandria, the Egyptians honoured Agathodaimon (the good spirit), a serpent god of fortune.

In African mythology, the snake is a symbol of royalty. There is a cult of the sacred python, and snakes are associated with fertility, rain, the rainbow, and thunder and lightning. The snake can be an incarnation of an ancestor and a guardian of treasure. It is also a culture hero who taught humanity smithcraft and agriculture. At Benin, one of the gods was a snake god called Danh.

In Haitian voodoo, the god Simbi is the patron deity of springs, rain, and magicians. His symbol is a snake. Ti-Jean Petro may also be a snake god; he is one-footed or footless (see Tiamat below). His origins are indigenous American rather than African.

In Sumerian mythology, Tiamat, the footless one, was the serpent of darkness, the great dragon, and the primordial sea. She was slain by Marduk, and he made the earth from her remains. The goddess Ishtar was said to be covered with scales like a snake. Joseph Campbell suggests that the Sumerians knew of the mysteries represented by the kundalini and the caduceus. The libation vase of King Gudea of Lagash (circa 2000 bce) had as its ornamentation a high relief of two cherubim or lion-birds guarding the door of a shrine to the Mesopotamian serpent god Ningishzida manifesting as a pair of copulating vipers entwined around a rod. Ningishzida was the lord of the Tree of Life. The whole picture resembles both the caduceus of Greek mythology and the seven chakras on the sushumna. The serpent was the main emblem of Sabazios, and his priestesses dropped golden serpents through their robes to symbolise the god within their bosom. The goddess Nidaba had snakes rising from her shoulders. She was the goddess of writing, education, science and account keeping, as well as a corn goddess. Writing first occurred in the form of pictographs in the temple of Inanna in Uruk; women were scribes, poets, scholars, and the authors of religious texts. In

Assyro-Babylonian myth, Ea is sometimes divided into Lakhmu and Lakhamu, male and female serpents giving birth to Anshar (the masculine principle or heaven) and Kishar (the feminine principle or earth). Lakhmu and Lakhamu were the offspring of Tiamat, and helped her in her battle against Marduk. Lakhmu was the personification of the primeval sediment, and was invoked on the completion of a building. Tiamat was the goddess of the salt sea, whilst Apsu, her consort, was the fresh waters of the land. Starhawk, in "Truth or Dare: Encounters with Power, Authority, and Mystery" shows how Mesopotamia was originally matrifocal, then gradually became more and more patriarchal with the emergence of warring city states competing for ever smaller areas of fertile land. During this process, the serpent goddesses of matrifocal antiquity became feared as manifestations of female power and mystery. An obvious example is the serpent of the Garden of Eden, but there is also the serpent of the forest called Khumbaba, slain by Gilgamesh. Ishtar is often depicted with a snake, and was viciously insulted by Gilgamesh in the "Epic of Gilgamesh". At the end of the epic, however, Gilgamesh has finally found the herb which bestows immortality, when it is stolen from him whilst he bathes by a serpent, who thereby gains the power to renew itself by shedding its skin.

> "Gilgamesh must die. The snake, however, has always been the symbol of the Goddess... In the end, all kings must die, but the great energies of life have the power to renew themselves and rise again."
> (Starhawk, op.cit., p.60)

The goddess Astarte (originally a Canaanite goddess) is depicted in an Egyptian relief standing on a lion, offering a lotus to the Egyptian god Min and serpents to the Canaanite god Reshef. Astarte was known to the Egyptians as Qodshu. Another snake goddess was Kadi, an Assyro-Babylonian deity worshipped at Der; she was portrayed as a snake with human breasts. The Dying God cults also depicted the god with serpents rising from his shoulders. In the Ophitic tradition, the Moon Goddess Cybele (whose consort was the dying god Attis) is engraved on their jewels offering a cup to a snake. In Canaan and Palestine, the serpent entwined upon a pole was worshipped as a god of healing, and also as a representation of the Earth Goddess. The symbolism of the Ophitic cults (from Greek ophis, a serpent) found its way into Christian tradition.

> "the persistent ophitic tradition... of Christ in the image of a serpent: not only in illustration of the Savior's words to Nicodemus the Pharisee, likening himself to the serpent of bronze elevated by Moses in the wilderness (Numbers 21, 5-9), but also in the Gnostic sense of an association of the messenger of salvation with the idea of the serpent in the Garden of Eden, who according to this way of inverting the orthodox interpretation, had been the first to attempt to release mankind from bondage to an unknowing god who had identified himself with the Absolute and thus blocked the way to the tree of eternal life."
>
> from "The Inner Reaches of Outer Space: Metaphor as Myth and as Religion" by Joseph Campbell

In Gnosticism, the snake is the manifestation of Sophia, goddess of wisdom, and the giver of gnosis. An excellent novel on this subject is 'The Wild Girl' by Michèle Roberts. Sophia is both the dove of the Holy Spirit and the serpent of wisdom. Phanes, the winged serpent, represents the light of the world, knowledge and illumination. He is depicted with golden wings and the heads of a ram, bull, snake, and lion (the tetramorphs). In the Orphic Tradition, Phanes was the first the first being to be born from the Cosmic Egg; his name means "he who appears"and is connected with the word phenomenon. The snake was also a symbol of Christ in Manichaeism. In Ireland, the serpent in the garden of Eden was regarded as feminine, and was known as the Nathair Parrthuis (the serpent of paradise). There may have been links between the Celtic Church in Ireland and Gnostic beliefs, via the Coptic Church.

In Zoroastrianism, the serpent Azidahaka was the demon who cut the first mortal in two. The first mortal was called Yima. (This legend bears an odd resemblance to the legend of the dismemberment of Ymir, the first being, by Oðinn, Vili, and Vé.)

The Great Goddess is frequently depicted with serpents, especially in Crete where she holds a serpent in each hand, both as a protection of the household and as a phallic symbol. There seems to be some evidence that there was a serpent cult in Crete; certainly snake symbolism is widespread there. The Great Goddess is depicted on ancient coins seated under a tree and caressing the head of a snake. The snake also appears in the cult of Eileithyia, goddess of childbirth. Serpents are associated with pregnancy in many mythologies, the serpent being regarded as the husband of all women. When associated with the Great Mother, the serpent takes on the connotations of secrecy, intuition, and mystery.

In Iranian mythology, the serpent is an aspect of Ahriman or Angra Mainyu, the Serpent of Darkness, the Liar. The snake Azi-dahak is the throttler, the enemy of the sun god. In Islam, the serpent is closely associated with life. It is called *el-hayyah*, and the word for life is el-hyat, whilst one of the names of God is El-Hay, which signifies the life-giving principle.

The serpent also twines around the cosmic tree in many mythologies. It is both the guardian of the tree, as in the legend of the Golden Fleece, and the initiator into its mysteries, as in the Kundalini serpent and the serpent of the Tree of the Knowledge of Good and Evil. Ultimately it symbolises energy rising from one level to another and transforming the individual in the process. It is also the cycles of dissolution and reintegration. On Yggdrasil, the World Tree, there are two serpents. Niðhögg lives in the underworld, the realm of the unmanifest, and represents the shadow self. Jörmungand lives in Midgard, and holds the ocean within his coils, maintaining order. In Hindu mythology, the churning of the primordial ocean occurred because the gods and demons had a tug of war with the serpent Vasuki, which was coiled around the world mountain (Mount Mandara). The churning of the ocean produced the liquid of immortality. The coiled serpent represents the cycles of manifestation. It sometimes appears (particularly in Orphic and Druidic mysteries) coiled round an egg, incubating the vital spirit. As the Ouroboros, it represents the waters encircling the earth. Two serpents twining round each other or biting each other's tails represent the ultimate unity of dualistic forces. Two snakes entwined represent Time and Fate. The serpent goddess Sarparajni is 'the mother of all that moves'.

Symbolism

Entwined snakes symbolise the dual creative forces within the world of forms. When twined round a staff, they form the caduceus, the staff of Hermes/Mercury. They are also a symbol of Asklepios, god of healing, because it was said that when old the serpent has the power of regenerating itself by casting its slough, which it was thought to do by squeezing itself between two rocks. It was also thought to have the ability to discover healing herbs. The two serpents on the staff represent illness and health, and the homeopathic properties of healing and poison. As snakes live underground, they are associated with the dead and the underworld, and are often depicted in funerary art, and associated with initiation. The snake can also represent the rays of the sun, its course across the heavens, and bolts of lightning. Most river deities are associated with snakes.

The serpent symbolised deity because it was believed to feed upon its own body, according to Plutarch, "even so all things spring from God, and will be resolved into deity again" (De Iside et Osiride). It also symbolised eternity, particularly in the form of the ouroboros, the serpent which forms a circle by holding its tail in its mouth. Serpents, large fish, and dragons all symbolise the Great Mother in her entwining and devouring aspect.

As a killer, the snake symbolises death and destruction. Since it renews its skin, it symbolises resurrection and life. When coiled, it represents the cycles of manifestation. It is both solar and lunar, and represents both light and darkness. The watchful, lidless eyes of the snake and other reptiles signify wisdom and awareness.

In Christianity the serpent generally represents evil, though it may represent wisdom: "Be ye therefore wise as serpents, and harmless as doves" (Matthew 10, 16). It also symbolises subtlety: "Now the serpent was more subtil than any beast of the field" (Genesis 3, 1). Usually, however, the serpent represents the temptation of Eve and Adam to eat the fruit of the Tree of the Knowledge of Good and Evil. In some stories, the snake is held to represent Paganism, as in the story that St Patrick banished all the snakes from Ireland. It also represents the devil as the tempter. Depicted beneath the cross of Christ, it represents Christ's triumph over the power of evil; crushed beneath the foot of the Virgin Mary, it is contrasted with the serpent of Eve. The early Christians called Christ 'the Good Serpent' because of his words to Nicodemus "And as Moses lifted up the serpent in the wilderness, so must the Son of Man be lifted up; that whoever believes in him may have eternal life" (John 3, 15). In the Book of Kells, the page illustrating Matthew 27:38 ("tunc crucifixerant cum eo duos latrones") is illuminated with twining serpents. A serpent twined around the Tree of life is beneficent; twined around the Tree of Knowledge, it is maleficent (unless in a Gnostic context). The chalice of St John is depicted with a serpent emerging from it, representing beneficent powers. At Monasterboice, Louth, Ireland, the Cross of Muiredach has carved upon it two interlocking serpents, one heading downward, the other upward. They enfold three human heads within their coils, and terminate in a human right hand reaching into a circle at the top, which resembles a halo or a solar disk. The carving is known as Dextra Dei, the right hand of God. According to the Gnostic Gospel of Thomas, Jesus said, "The Pharisees and the Scribes have received the keys of Knowledge, they have hidden them. They did not enter, and they did not let those enter who wished. But you, become wise as serpents and innocent as doves." (Logion 39)

In Judaism, the snake represents evil, temptation, sin, sexual passion, and the souls of the damned in Sheol. Lightning is referred to as 'the crooked serpent' (Job 26, 13). The brazen serpent of Moses is regarded as a healing symbol. In Kabbalah, Adam Kadmon, the primordial man, is depicted holding a serpent by the neck.

In Egyptian art, sovereigns are depicted with the uraeus, the symbol of sovereignty, royalty, power, light, life and death, the eye of Ra, and the destruction of enemies. The uraeus, a cobra, represented the divine royal power and wisdom, whilst the coluber represented Set and Apep as the demon of darkness and the malefic aspect of the midday sun. A representation of the uraeus was worn on the front of the crown of Egypt. A snake with a lion's head gave protection from evil.

The thirteenth sign of the Zodiac is Ophiuchus, the serpent-bearer. The constellation lies slightly outside the ecliptic, and it is therefore uncertain whether or not it is part of the Zodiac. If the Western tradition used a lunar calendar, it might have been included.

As a cthonic creature, the serpent is traditionally an enemy of the solar birds, such as the eagle, crane, and heron. Birds are of the heavens and the realms of spirit, whereas snakes are earthy, representing the dynamism, urges, and energies of the element of Earth. Most lunar and cthonic deities can be represented as a snake, or have a snake as their attribute.

Poetry

Wisdom of serpent be thine,
Wisdom of raven be thine,

Wisdom of valiant eagle.

Voice of swan be thine,
Voice of honey be thine,
Voice of the son of the stars.

Bounty of sea be thine,
Bounty of land be thine,
Bounty of the Father of Heaven.

(Gaelic blessing from the *Carmina Gadelica*)

I will voyage in God's name
In likeness of deer, in likeness of horse,
In likeness of serpent, in likeness of king.
More powerful will it be with me than with all others.

(Gaelic charm from the *Carmina Gadelica*)

Tortoise

Varieties

The tortoise and the turtle were not distinguished before the sixteenth century, so many mythologies regard them as interchangeable. The Greek Tortoise (*Testudo graeca*) is found in the region of the Mediterranean. There are several species of Giant Tortoise (*Testudo gigantica*), which come from the Galapagos Islands. The Margined Tortoise (*Testudo marginata*) is found in south-eastern Europe and Asia Minor. The Spurred Tortoise (*Testudo sulcata*) is found in Africa. The Four-toed Tortoise (*Testudo horsfieldii*) is found from the western Caspian region, through central Asia, as far as western Pakistan. The Red-footed Tortoise (*Testudo carbonaria*) is a South American species, and has a black carapace with yellow markings. The Forest Hinged Tortoise (*Kinyxis erosa*) is found in tropical West Africa; it has a divided carapace. The Radiated Tortoise (*Testudo radiata*) is found in Madagascar. The scariest-looking Tortoise is a South American carnivorous species called Matamata (*Chelys fimbriata*).

Folklore

According to Greek legend, the tortoise could hatch its eggs just by looking at them.

The Chinese made stone tortoises with large slabs on their backs; this was a form of sympathetic magic to prevent earthquakes and bring the celestial and terrestrial realms closer together.

Mythology

The tortoise represents the waters, the Moon, the Earth Mother, creation, time, immortality, fertility, and regeneration. It is regarded as the sustainer of everything and the support of the earth.

In Hindu mythology, the tortoise Chukwa supports the elephant Maha-pudma, which upholds the world. (The elephant is a masculine power, the tortoise feminine; together they represent the potential for life.) In another legend, the tortoise Akupera supports the world on its back. Kasyapa, the North Star, was the first living creature, and the progenitor of all life (he was a tortoise). He was the husband of Vinata, the sister of the queen of the serpents (one of the Nagas). He was an avatar of Vishnu, the Preserver and the Power of the Waters. His lower shell is the earth, and his upper shell is the heavens. Kasyapa and Vinata were the parents of Garuda, the divine bird-man and steed of Vishnu. Kasyapa was one of the seven great Rishis or sages. In another myth cycle he was married to Diti, the goddess of infinity, and she gave birth to the Daityas (the Vedic equivalent of the Titans) and the Maruts (the companions of Rudra, the storm god). Kasyapa's titles are the Old Tortoise Man and the Lord Progenitor of All Creatures. The second avatar of Vishnu was also a tortoise; he was called Kurma, and he dived to the bottom of the ocean to recover the treasures of the Vedic tribes which were lost in the great flood.

In China, the tortoise is regarded as one of the Four Spiritually Endowed (or Auspicious) Creatures (the others being the dragon, the phoenix, and the unicorn). It represents the North, Yin, and the element of Water. It is known as the Black Warrior, and denotes strength, endurance, and primordial chaos. It was believed to live for a long time and hence it was a symbol of longevity. In Chinese cosmology, the tortoise supports the world, and the four corners of the earth are its four feet. In Taoism, it represents the great triad of the heavens, the earth, and the waters: the dome of its back is the sky, its body is the earth, and its lower shell is the waters. The imperial army carried tortoise and dragon banners to represent indestructibility, because neither can destroy the other: the dragon cannot crush the tortoise and the tortoise cannot reach the dragon. The goddess Hsi-wang-mu (see Toad) is also known as the Golden Mother of the Tortoise. The shell of the tortoise can be used in divination.

In Japan, the Cosmic Mountain and the dwelling of the Sennin (the Taoist Immortals) are supported by a tortoise. It is also an attribute of Kumpira, the god of sailors, and of Benten, the goddess of the sea. Benten was mainly worshipped on the outlying islands of Japan; there was a shrine to her at Enoshim, where she was said to have enchanted and married a dragon which was devouring the children of the area. She was one of the seven deities of good luck, the Shichi Fukujin. The tortoise is also an attribute of Fukurokuju, the god of wisdom and longevity, and of Jorojin, the god of longevity and good luck.

In Graeco-Roman myth, the tortoise was regarded as the feminine power of the waters, and was associated with Venus and Aphrodite, who was born from the sea. It was also an emblem of Hermes and Mercury. According to Pausanias it was sacred to Pan in Arcadia, and it was forbidden to kill it. (There are wild tortoises in Greece.)

In indigenous American mythology, the tortoise and the turtle are interchangeable. The continent of America was known as Turtle Island. In Lakota (Sioux) myth, the world is a huge turtle floating on the waters. In Huron cosmology, the tortoise supports the world. There are various turtle clans and the people of the Pueblos hold turtle dances in spring and autumn. The tortoise and the turtle are associated with the earth and the waters, and the feminine power. In some legends, the cosmic tree grows out of the tortoise's back. Among the Maidu of California, the god Talvolte was the head of a tortoise clan and one of the survivors of the deluge.

In Mexico, the tortoise was the Great Mother in her terrible aspect.

In West African mythology, the tortoise gave ju-ju to humanity, and it is incorporated into fertility rituals. The tortoise is sometimes a trickster figure, but it is always outwitted. Like Brer Rabbit and Anansi, tortoise stories were taken to the Caribbean from Africa.

In ancient Egypt, the sign of Libra was associated with two tortoises, as the measure of the flood waters of the Nile.

In Sumer, the tortoise was sacred to Ea-Oannes as Lord of the Great Deep.

Symbolism

The tortoise is generally regarded as a manifestation of feminine power, and is associated with the element of Water.

The tortoise typifies plodding persistence. In the fable of the hare and the tortoise, the tortoise wins because it plods along till it gets to the end of the course, whereas the hare doesn't bother to start till later because it is so sure that it will win, and it loses.

The name tortoise (*testudo* in Latin) was given to the battle formation where soldiers placed their rectangular shields over their heads to attack a fort.

In Alchemy, the tortoise symbolised the massa confusa.

In Christianity the tortoise was a symbol of the chaste wife living retired in the house. In early Christian art it, however, it was a symbol of evil, as opposed to the cockerel of vigilance.

Turtle

Deities	Hsuan-T'ien Shang-ti, Ao
Element	Water
Polarity	Yin
Order	Chelonidae
Etymology	apparently an alternative version of tortue (see tortoise), assimilated to turtle (as in turtle-dove)

Varieties

Turtles belong to the order *Chelonia*. The Hawksbill (*Eretmochelys imbricata*) and the Green or Edible Turtle (*Chelonia mydas*) are found in warm seas. The European Pond Turtle (*Emys orbicularis*), found as far north as Holland and Lithuania, may live to be a hundred years old. The Eastern Box Turtle (*Terrapene carolina*) is a terrestrial turtle from America. An aquatic turtle from America is the False Map Turtle (*Graptemys pseudogeographica*). The Snapping Turtle (*Chelydra serpentina*) lives in the rivers and marshes of North America, east of the Rockies. The Alligator Snapping Turtle (*Macroclemys temminckii*) is a larger version of the Snapping Turtle, and inhabits the same geographical area and habitat. The sub-order Trionychoidea includes the African Soft-shelled Turtle (*Trionyx triunguis*), which is found in the swamps of equatorial Africa, and as far north as Egypt and Syria. A related species from China, *Trionyx sinensis*, used to be regarded as a sacred animal; it has a strange pointy snout.

Mythology

In China, the turtle is an attribute of the god of examinations. The deity Hsuan-T'ien Shang-ti (Great Lord of the Dark Heaven) is depicted standing barefoot on a turtle surrounded by a snake. Hsuan-T'ien Shang-ti is the enemy of demons and the Regent of Water. The cosmic mountain is sometimes represented as a sea turtle in Chinese mythology. The turtle/mountain is called Ao. The goddess Nü-gua repaired one of the four pillars which support the earth with one of the turtle's legs. The earth itself was believed to be supported by a huge turtle or tortoise (q.v.).

Among the Hopi, the turtle is never teased, molested, or eaten, because the turtle katsina, Yonyosona, is a helpful spirit, associated with water and rain. Turtles are sometimes 'sent home' to the spirit world so that their shells can be used as leg rattles for the dancers in the katsina ceremonies.

The Kakadu people of Van Arnhem land in Australia have a culture hero called Muraian, who is known as the Turtle Man.

In Egypt, the turtle represented drought, and was an enemy of the sun god.

Symbolism

The turtle is a phallic symbol, and represents lubricity, slowness, and longevity.

Among the Maoris, the turtle was known as the land-worker, and symbolised agriculture and a successful harvest.

To indigenous Americans, the turtle symbolises cowardliness, bragging, sensuality, obscenity, earthiness, and Winter. These things are also symbolised by the leech.

Literature

In Terry Pratchett's *Discworld* series, the world is supported by a turtle called Great A'Tuin. No-one knows if it is male or female. Legend has it that it is swimming through space to mate on the shores of some distant galaxy. Presumably there will be some kind of cataclysm when this happens....

Many of the indigenous peoples of America referred to their continent as Turtle Island.

A Hoysala sculpture of a Naga couple. Halebidu.
http://commons.wikimedia.org/wiki/File:Naga182.JPG